LIGHTNING, LIBRARIES, AND LIBERTY

THE STORY OF BENJAMIN FRANKLIN FOR KIDS

SARAH MICHAELS

BOOKSTEM

Copyright © 2025 by Sarah Michaels

All rights reserved.

No part of this book may be reproduced in any form or by any electronic or mechanical means, including information storage and retrieval systems, without written permission from the author, except for the use of brief quotations in a book review.

1

MEET BENJAMIN FRANKLIN

Benjamin Franklin was a man who seemed to do everything. He was a printer, a writer, a scientist, an inventor, a businessman, and a leader in the fight for American independence. He didn't come from a wealthy family, and he didn't have much formal schooling, but that didn't stop him from becoming one of the most influential people in history.

He was born in Boston in 1706, the fifteenth of seventeen children. Life in a big family meant sharing everything—food, clothes, space, and chores. His father, Josiah Franklin, made soap and candles, and he expected his sons to help in the family business. But young Ben had no interest in spending his days melting tallow and dipping wicks. He wanted to read, learn, and explore new ideas.

Books fascinated him. At a time when many children didn't even know how to read, he devoured every book he could find. When his father decided that Ben should become a preacher, he sent him to school. But money was tight, and after only two years, Ben's formal education ended. That didn't stop him. If he couldn't go to school, he would teach himself.

By the age of 12, Ben had a job as an apprentice at his older brother James's print shop. It was hard work—long hours spent setting type, operating the press, and delivering newspapers around town. His brother could be strict, but Ben didn't mind. The shop gave him access to more books. At night, after the work was done, he would borrow books from local merchants, reading late into the night before returning them early in the morning.

Printing wasn't just about books. It was also about news, ideas, and opinions. His brother's newspaper, *The New-England Courant*, often printed bold and controversial opinions about the government and society. Ben wanted to write for the paper, but James wouldn't let him. A 16-year-old apprentice wasn't exactly a respected journalist.

Instead of giving up, Ben came up with a clever plan.

Under the name "Silence Dogood," he wrote a series of letters and secretly slipped them under the print shop door. The letters were full of humor and sharp observations about life in the colonies. People loved them. No one knew the witty writer behind the letters was actually a teenager. When James finally found out, he wasn't happy. He had no interest in letting his younger brother share the spotlight. The two argued, and eventually, Ben had enough. He decided it was time to leave.

At 17, he packed up and ran away to Philadelphia. He arrived with almost no money, no job, and no place to stay. But he wasn't the type to sit around feeling sorry for himself. He found work at a printing shop, made friends, and before long, his hard work started to pay off. He traveled to England to learn more about printing, then returned to Philadelphia and started his own print shop.

Printing gave Ben a way to earn a living, but it also gave him a way to spread ideas. He published *The Pennsylvania Gazette*, one of the most popular newspapers in the colonies. Then he started *Poor Richard's Almanack*, a yearly book filled with weather forecasts, advice, and clever sayings like "A penny saved is a penny earned." These sayings, called proverbs, were easy to remember and packed with wisdom. People still use many of them today.

But Ben wasn't just a printer. He had a mind that was always full of questions. Why did lightning strike certain places more than others? Could there be a way to harness electricity? How could fires be prevented in growing cities? He wanted to solve problems, and when he saw something that needed improving, he got to work.

One of his most famous inventions was the lightning rod. At the time, people didn't understand much about electricity, and lightning was a dangerous mystery. Buildings often caught fire when they were struck. Through experiments, Ben discovered that a metal rod placed on top of a building could safely guide lightning into the ground, preventing fires.

That wasn't his only invention. He created bifocal glasses so he wouldn't have to switch between two pairs of lenses. He designed a more efficient stove to help people heat their homes with less wood. He even invented a musical instrument called the glass armonica, which composers like Beethoven and Mozart later used in their music.

Beyond inventing, Ben believed in improving the

world around him. He helped start the first public library, organized the first volunteer fire department, and worked to make the postal system more efficient. He believed that knowledge should be shared and that communities worked best when people helped one another.

As he got older, his curiosity didn't fade, but his interests expanded. He became involved in politics, helping the American colonies as they struggled for independence from Britain. He helped write the Declaration of Independence, traveled to France to gain support for the war, and later played a major role in shaping the U.S. Constitution. His wisdom and experience made him one of the most respected voices of his time.

By the time he passed away in 1790, he had left behind a legacy of inventions, discoveries, and ideas that still shape the world today. He wasn't born into wealth or power. He didn't have the advantage of a long education. But through curiosity, hard work, and a love of learning, he became one of the most remarkable figures in history.

Why he is an important figure in history

One of the biggest reasons Franklin stands out in history is that he believed in progress. He saw problems and worked to fix them. During his time, most people accepted things the way they were. If streets were dark at night, they just dealt with it. If letters took weeks to arrive, that was just the way things worked. Franklin refused to accept that things couldn't be improved. He introduced ideas that changed everyday life, making it safer, more efficient, and more connected.

His work in science is one of the things people admire most. Before Franklin's experiments, lightning was a mystery. People feared it, and churches were often the tallest buildings in town, making them frequent targets. Fires started, and there was little anyone could do to stop them. Franklin's curiosity led him to study electricity, and he realized that lightning was a powerful force of nature—not magic, as some believed. His invention of the lightning rod gave buildings protection for the first time. It may seem simple now, but at the time, it was a major breakthrough that saved lives and property.

Electricity wasn't his only area of interest. He studied weather patterns, ocean currents, and even the common cold. His discoveries helped people understand the world around them better. He noticed that ships traveling from Europe to America took longer than those going in the opposite direction. This led him to study the Gulf Stream, an ocean current that affects travel and trade even today. Many of his observations are still used in science, showing how one person's curiosity can lead to discoveries that last for centuries.

Franklin wasn't just focused on science—he believed in building strong communities. He helped establish the first public library in America because he wanted more people to have access to books, not just the wealthy. He knew knowledge was powerful, and he wanted to share it. He also created the first volunteer fire department in Philadelphia because fires were a constant danger in wooden cities. Instead of waiting for someone else to solve problems, he took action, bringing people together to work for the common good.

His influence extended beyond the city and into the entire country. Franklin played a key role in the American Revolution. Before the United States was a country, the American colonies were ruled by Great Britain. The British government made laws and collected taxes, but the colonists had no say in the decisions. Franklin originally hoped the colonies and Britain could work out their differences peacefully, but as tensions grew, he realized that wasn't possible. He joined others in calling for independence, becoming one of the leaders who shaped the new nation.

When the colonies decided to break away from Britain, Franklin helped write the Declaration of Independence. This was not just another document—it was a bold statement that the colonies were no longer under British rule. It explained why they deserved to govern themselves. Franklin's support and wisdom helped guide the process, and his signature is one of the most famous on the document.

After independence was declared, the colonies faced a huge challenge—winning the war against the powerful British army. Franklin was too old to fight on the battlefield, but he helped in other ways. He traveled to France to convince the French government to help America. At the time, France and Britain were rivals, and Franklin used his charm, intelligence, and reputation to persuade France to send money, troops, and supplies. This support played a major role in helping the colonies win the war.

Even after the war, Franklin continued to shape

the new country. When leaders gathered to create the U.S. Constitution, he was there to offer advice and ideas. His experience, both in America and overseas, made him one of the most respected voices in the room. He encouraged compromise, knowing that different opinions had to be balanced to create a strong and lasting government. The system of government created in the Constitution is still in place today, proving how important Franklin's role was.

Beyond his work in science, invention, and government, Franklin's writing continues to influence people. His book *Poor Richard's Almanack* wasn't just a calendar; it was full of advice and wisdom. Sayings like "Early to bed and early to rise makes a man healthy, wealthy, and wise" and "Well done is better than well said" have been repeated for generations. These weren't just catchy phrases—they reflected Franklin's beliefs about hard work, self-improvement, and making the most of opportunities.

2

YOUNG BEN – THE BOY WHO LOVED TO READ

Benjamin Franklin grew up in a house that was never quiet. With seventeen children in the family, there was always someone talking, working, or running around. It was the kind of place where privacy didn't exist, and there was always a line to get food at the dinner table. Every morning started early, and every night ended with someone still finishing chores.

His father, Josiah Franklin, worked as a candle and soap maker, and that meant long days of melting tallow, dipping wicks, and pouring hot wax into molds. It wasn't an easy business, but it provided enough to support the large family. Even with everyone pitching in, there were still plenty of challenges. Money was tight, food had to stretch to feed everyone, and there wasn't much room for extra comforts.

The Franklin home on Milk Street in Boston was small for such a big family. Space was always a problem, and Ben shared a bed with several of his brothers. In the winter, that wasn't too bad—it helped keep them warm. But in the summer, it was crowded and uncomfortable. There was no such thing as personal space. Every inch of the house was used for something, whether it was storing supplies, cooking meals, or getting work done.

Meals were simple. The family ate a lot of bread, porridge, and stews because they were cheap and easy to make in large batches. Fresh meat was a rare treat, and fish was a common meal since Boston was a busy port city. Ben didn't mind simple food, and as he got older, he became even more interested in eating in a way that saved money and kept him healthy. He eventually chose to follow a mostly vegetarian diet, which helped him spend less on meals and more on books.

With so many children, Josiah Franklin expected everyone to work. There were no lazy days, and everyone had a role to play. Whether it was helping in the candle shop, fetching water, or running errands, there was always something to do. From an early age, Ben was given tasks to help keep the household running. He wasn't afraid of hard work, but his interests were different from many of his siblings. While others focused on learning trades or helping in the shop, Ben was drawn to books.

Reading became one of the most important things in his life. Books weren't easy to come by, especially in a large family where buying them wasn't a priority. He borrowed them whenever he could, reading anything he could get his hands on. He didn't just read for fun—he read to learn.

At the time, most children in the colonies didn't go to school for long. Learning to read and write was considered important, but once a child could do that, they were usually expected to start working. Josiah Franklin had originally hoped that Ben would become a minister, so he sent him to the Boston Latin School. He did well, but after only two years, his formal education ended because the family couldn't afford to keep sending him.

That didn't stop him from learning. He came up with his own ways to continue his education. He studied books on his own, practicing writing by copying essays word for word and then trying to rewrite them from memory. He paid attention to how arguments were structured, how words were used, and how ideas were explained. If he came across a word he didn't know, he looked it up and made sure to remember it.

Unlike many kids his age, he enjoyed reading difficult books. He wanted to understand philosophy, science, and history. He didn't just accept what was written—he asked questions about it. He debated ideas in his head and sometimes with others, always trying to make sense of the world around him.

His love of books shaped the way he thought about life. He believed that knowledge should be shared, and that's something he carried with him throughout his entire life. Later, when he was older and more successful, he helped start the first public library in America. He knew what it was like to struggle to find books, and he wanted to make sure other people had access to them.

Being part of such a large family taught him many things. It taught him patience, since there was always someone talking over him or taking the last piece of bread. It taught him how to work hard, since no one in the Franklin house could afford to be lazy. And it taught him that if he wanted something different for his life, he would have to create his own opportunities.

His brothers and sisters followed more traditional paths, learning trades and staying in Boston. Ben, however, had bigger plans. He knew that if he wanted to learn more, see more, and do more, he would have to find his own way. Reading opened his mind to possibilities beyond what his family expected of him. It showed him that there was more to the world than making candles and soap.

His love for books and learning

Books weren't just something Benjamin Franklin enjoyed—they were the key to everything he wanted to learn. At a time when most kids in the American colonies had little access to books, he found ways to read as much as possible. He didn't read to pass the time or for entertainment. He read to understand, to question, and to expand his knowledge.

From an early age, he realized that books were filled with ideas from people who had lived before him. They held lessons, discoveries, and ways of thinking that could help him become smarter and more capable. He didn't have tutors or a long formal education, but books gave him access to the knowledge of the world.

Finding books wasn't easy. Unlike today, there

were no public libraries where anyone could walk in and borrow a book. Books were expensive, and most families only owned a few. His family couldn't afford to buy them, but that didn't stop him. He borrowed books whenever he could. He would ask friends, neighbors, and even shop owners if they had books he could read. He treated books with care, knowing that if he damaged them, he might not get the chance to borrow again.

He also found creative ways to get more time with books. Since he worked at his brother James's print shop as an apprentice, he had access to reading materials that most kids his age didn't. Printing required setting type, pressing ink onto paper, and binding pages together, which meant that every book and newspaper that came through the shop passed through his hands.

When the workday ended, he didn't rush off to play. Instead, he stayed behind, reading everything he could. If he couldn't take a book home, he read as much as possible while he had access to it. He studied newspapers, essays, and books on a wide range of topics, from history and philosophy to science and politics.

His learning didn't stop at reading—he practiced writing, too. He wanted to improve the way he expressed ideas, so he came up with a system. He copied passages from books and then tried to rewrite them in his own words. Later, he would compare his writing to the original to see where he could improve. If a passage seemed especially well-written, he studied the way the author used words and structured sentences.

One of the books that influenced him the most was *The Pilgrim's Progress* by John Bunyan. It was a popular book at the time, and Franklin read it so often that he practically memorized it. He also admired the works of famous essayists and thinkers, including the writings of the ancient Greek philosophers. Even though these texts were difficult, he pushed himself to understand them.

As he grew older, his interest in learning only deepened. He didn't just want to read about ideas—he wanted to discuss them. He sought out people who were well-educated and enjoyed debating. Since he was still young, not everyone took him seriously at first, but his sharp thinking and knowledge gained him respect.

To further challenge himself, he developed a habit of questioning everything he read. If an author made a claim, Franklin didn't just accept it as fact. He asked whether it made sense and considered other perspectives. If he disagreed with something, he thought about how he would argue against it. This way of thinking helped shape the way he approached life. He never accepted things just because others did—he needed to understand them for himself.

Working in his brother's print shop

At twelve years old, he became an apprentice at James Franklin's print shop in Boston. Apprenticeships were a common way for young people to learn a trade, but they weren't easy. Apprentices worked long hours for little or no pay, and they had to do whatever their master required of them. For Ben, that meant years of hard work, with no choice but to obey his older brother. The apprenticeship was supposed to last until he turned twenty-one.

The print shop was a busy place, filled with the smell of ink and the sound of heavy wooden presses at work. Printing in the early 1700s wasn't like printing today. There were no computers, no automatic machines—everything had to be done by hand. Each letter had to be set into place one at a time, pages had to be inked, and then they were pressed onto paper using large, heavy printing presses. It was slow, tiring work, and Ben was responsible for many of the most difficult tasks.

His days started early. There were papers to fold, ink to mix, and type to set. He had to prepare the presses, carry heavy trays of metal letters, and sometimes even deliver newspapers around town. Printing wasn't just about putting words on paper—it was a physical job that required strength and stamina. He spent hours hunched over, carefully arranging tiny pieces of type into sentences and paragraphs. One mistake meant having to start over.

Even though the work was exhausting, Ben found ways to make the most of his time. Being surrounded by words all day gave him a chance to learn more. He read everything that passed through the shop—newspapers, pamphlets, essays, and books. He wasn't just printing words; he was studying them. He paid attention to how arguments were made, how opinions were expressed, and how sentences were structured.

At the time, James Franklin published a newspaper called *The New-England Courant*. Unlike most newspapers, which were controlled by the government or religious groups, James's paper was different. It was bold, opinionated, and often controversial. It criticized local leaders and questioned authority, which made it both popular and risky.

Ben wanted to contribute. He was eager to write for the paper, but James wouldn't let him. No one wanted to read the thoughts of a teenage apprentice, and James wasn't about to give his younger brother a voice in his publication. Ben wasn't discouraged. Instead, he came up with a plan.

If he couldn't get published under his own name, he would do it under someone else's. He created a fake identity—Silence Dogood, a fictional widow with strong opinions and a sharp sense of humor. Writing as Silence Dogood, he slipped essays under the print shop door at night, pretending they were letters from a concerned citizen. James and the other printers, thinking they had stumbled upon something valuable, published the letters in the paper.

The Silence Dogood letters became popular. People enjoyed the witty observations and clever criticism of colonial society. They debated who the mysterious writer might be. No one suspected that the person behind the words was a teenage apprentice. When Ben finally revealed that he was Silence Dogood, James wasn't amused. Instead of being impressed, he was angry.

Their relationship, already tense, became worse.

James wasn't the easiest person to work for. He was strict, demanding, and often harsh. He didn't appreciate being outshined by his younger brother, and their arguments became more frequent. Ben knew he couldn't stay in the print shop forever. He had learned the trade, but he wanted more than what James was willing to give him.

3
RUNNING AWAY TO PHILADELPHIA

Benjamin Franklin wasn't someone who accepted limits. If a door was closed, he found another way in. If a rule seemed unfair, he questioned it. That attitude had served him well when he tricked his brother James into publishing his Silence Dogood letters, but it also made his apprenticeship more difficult.

James Franklin was not an easy person to work for. He was demanding, strict, and quick-tempered. Being an apprentice meant long hours of hard labor with little freedom. But it wasn't just the work that made things difficult—James was determined to keep Ben in his place. No matter how talented he was, he would always be the younger brother.

Tension between the two had been building for

years. At first, James had control over him simply because of the apprenticeship contract. As long as Ben was bound to it, he had no choice but to do what James said. But after the Silence Dogood incident, things became worse. James was furious when he learned that Ben had been writing under a fake name and had managed to fool him. Instead of being proud of his brother's cleverness, he was embarrassed.

Their arguments became more frequent, and James treated him even more harshly. It wasn't just about discipline anymore—it was about keeping Ben from thinking he was more important than he was. James refused to give him credit for his intelligence, refused to let him write for the paper under his own name, and refused to acknowledge that Ben was more than just an apprentice.

There were other problems, too. James's newspaper, *The New-England Courant*, had a habit of criticizing the government, and this got him into trouble. At one point, James was arrested for printing articles that offended local officials. During his time in jail, Ben kept the paper running. He had been working in the shop for years and knew how to do everything himself. The experience gave him a taste of what it would be like to run his own print shop, to be in charge of what got published.

But even after James was released, things didn't improve. James still refused to give Ben more freedom, and the frustration grew. Ben knew that staying in Boston meant spending the next several years working under his brother, with no chance to write, no chance to improve his situation, and no chance to control his own future.

He wanted something different.

Leaving wasn't as simple as quitting. An apprentice contract was legally binding, and James wasn't about to let him go. If Ben walked away, he could be arrested for breaking the agreement. That meant if he was going to leave, he had to do it carefully.

He came up with a plan. To get out of the contract without facing punishment, he and James agreed to tear it up. But James, still wanting to control him, never made it official. That meant Ben was free—but only in secret. If anyone found out, he could still be forced to return to his brother.

That was enough reason to leave Boston entirely. If he stayed, he would always be looking over his shoulder. He needed to go somewhere new, somewhere he could build a life for himself without his brother controlling him.

Philadelphia seemed like the best option. It was a growing city with opportunities in printing, and it was far enough from Boston that James couldn't interfere.

At seventeen years old, he packed up and left. He didn't have much money, and he had no job waiting for him when he arrived. But he was confident that he could make it work.

Journey to Philadelphia

Traveling in the early 1700s wasn't easy. There were no trains, no cars, and no direct routes between cities. The roads that did exist were rough, and most people traveled by foot, horseback, or boat. The fastest way to get from Boston to Philadelphia was by sea, but Franklin didn't have enough money for a direct passage. Instead, he took a series of smaller trips, working his way south bit by bit.

His first stop was New York City. It was a smaller city than Boston at the time, but it was still busy with trade, merchants, and ships constantly arriving and departing. He hoped to find work at a print shop there, but after speaking with the local printers, he realized there were no jobs available. That meant moving on.

The next destination was New Jersey, and getting there wasn't simple. Franklin had to board a boat, travel along rough waters, and walk long stretches of land to continue his journey. He was exhausted, hungry, and running out of money, but he refused to turn back.

When he reached Burlington, New Jersey, he was out of food and nearly broke. He managed to find bread from a local baker, using what little money he had left. He didn't have a place to sleep, no comfortable lodging, and no one to turn to for help. Every step of the journey was a test of his endurance.

From Burlington, he finally made his way to Philadelphia. When he arrived, he was dirty, tired, and wearing clothes that were wrinkled and messy from travel. He had walked for miles, spent days on boats, and had barely eaten enough to keep himself going. Despite all of this, he had made it.

Starting a new life in a new city

Arriving in Philadelphia was only the first step. Benjamin Franklin had escaped his brother's control in Boston, but he wasn't stepping into an easy life. He had no home, no job, and barely any money. He was in an unfamiliar city with no one to turn to, no safety net, and no clear plan other than finding work as a printer.

Philadelphia in the early 1700s was a busy place. It was larger than Boston, with a diverse population that included English settlers, German immigrants, and Quakers who had founded the city. The streets were filled with merchants selling goods, ships unloading cargo, and craftsmen working in their shops. Franklin took in the sights, knowing that if he wanted to survive here, he had to move quickly.

The first thing he needed was food. He had just enough money to buy a few rolls from a local baker. It wasn't much, but it gave him enough energy to start looking for work. He knew that the sooner he found a printing shop, the sooner he could start earning money.

He asked around and was eventually directed to the print shop of a man named Samuel Keimer. It wasn't the most successful shop in the city, but Keimer was willing to give Franklin a chance. The work was familiar—setting type, operating the press, and handling printed materials. It wasn't easy, but Franklin was used to long hours in a print shop. More importantly, he now had a way to earn a living.

Even with a job, he still had no permanent place to stay. He found temporary lodging at a boarding house, a common option for people who didn't have families in the city. These houses were crowded, filled with travelers, workers, and people looking for opportunities. It wasn't comfortable, but it was better than having no roof over his head.

Philadelphia's print industry wasn't as competitive as Boston's, but it was still difficult to stand out. Franklin worked hard, proving himself to be reliable, intelligent, and skilled at his trade. He wasn't just another worker—he had ideas, and he wasn't afraid to share them. Even though he was only seventeen, he quickly gained a reputation as someone who understood printing, writing, and business.

While working for Keimer, he met influential people in the city, including Andrew Bradford, who ran another print shop. Bradford's shop was more established than Keimer's, but he didn't have an immediate job available. Still, Franklin's skills caught his attention. Having multiple printers aware of his talents meant that he had more chances for future opportunities.

4

THE PRINTER AND THE WRITER

Printing wasn't just a job for Benjamin Franklin—it was the skill that gave him independence. It was how he earned money, how he connected with important people, and eventually, how he spread his ideas. He had spent years working under his brother James in Boston, setting type, running the press, and folding newspapers. When he arrived in Philadelphia, he was still young, but he already had more printing experience than most.

At first, he worked for Samuel Keimer, a printer who had a shop in the city. Keimer wasn't the best businessman, and his shop wasn't as well-run as Franklin thought it could be. But it was a start. It gave Franklin a chance to prove himself, and more importantly, it kept him working in a trade he knew well.

Printing was hard work. It wasn't just about putting ink on paper. Every letter had to be arranged by hand. If a word was misspelled, the entire section had to be reset. Ink had to be mixed to the right consistency, paper had to be prepared, and the heavy wooden press had to be operated with care. The process was slow, but it was the best way to produce newspapers, books, and pamphlets at the time.

Even though Keimer was the shop owner, Franklin quickly became one of the most knowledgeable printers there. He had a sharp eye for detail and understood how to make the press more efficient. His experience gave him an advantage, and it didn't take long before people in Philadelphia noticed that he was skilled at his craft.

While working at Keimer's shop, he met several important figures in the city. One of them was William Keith, the governor of Pennsylvania. Keith was impressed with Franklin's intelligence and work ethic. He believed Franklin had the potential to run his own printing business and offered to help him get started.

At first, the opportunity seemed perfect. Keith promised to support Franklin, telling him that if he traveled to London, he could buy printing equipment and return to Philadelphia ready to start his own shop. Franklin trusted him. Without questioning the plan, he set off for England, expecting to find letters of credit waiting for him when he arrived.

But when he reached London, he realized he had been misled. Keith hadn't sent any letters or money. Franklin was stranded in a foreign city with no job, no connections, and no way to start his own printing business. He had two choices: give up or find work.

He found a job at a London print shop, where he continued to refine his skills. London had some of the best printers in the world, and Franklin learned new techniques while working alongside experienced craftsmen. The shops in London were much larger than the ones in Philadelphia, and the work was even more demanding. But he adapted, using the opportunity to grow as a printer.

Living in London gave him a different perspective on printing. He saw how newspapers and books were used to spread ideas, challenge authority, and shape public opinion. He realized that printing wasn't just about producing words on paper—it was about influence. He wanted to do more than just print; he wanted to write.

After more than a year in London, Franklin returned to Philadelphia. He was older, more experienced, and more determined than ever. He had been tricked by Governor Keith, but instead of letting it ruin him, he used the experience to push himself forward. He knew that if he wanted to succeed, he couldn't rely on empty promises from powerful people—he had to build his future himself.

Publishing *Poor Richard's Almanack*

Benjamin Franklin had spent years learning the printing trade, working for others, and studying the business of printing. By the time he was in his late twenties, he had established himself as one of the most successful printers in Philadelphia. He was no longer just a worker in someone else's shop—he was running his own business.

Printing was more than a way to make money. It was a way to spread information, entertain, and educate people. Franklin had always been drawn to writing, and he knew that the most successful printers weren't just the ones who printed other people's words. They were the ones who created their own publications. He had already started *The Pennsylvania Gazette*, a newspaper that had quickly become popular. But newspapers only reached a certain audience, mostly those who were interested in politics and current events. Franklin wanted to create something that could reach an even larger group of people—something practical, useful, and entertaining.

In 1732, he introduced *Poor Richard's Almanack*. Almanacs were popular at the time because they provided everyday information that people needed. They included weather predictions, farming advice, calendars, and useful tips for daily life. Many people relied on them to plan their planting seasons and know what to expect from the year ahead. Franklin saw an opportunity to make his own version—one that would be both informative and filled with wisdom and humor.

Instead of publishing it under his own name, he created the character of Richard Saunders, or "Poor Richard." He made up a backstory for Poor Richard, presenting him as a simple but wise man who offered advice and observations on life. Franklin used this character to share proverbs, jokes, and lessons in a way that people would enjoy reading.

The almanac was filled with sayings that were easy to remember, like:

- "A penny saved is a penny earned."
- "Early to bed and early to rise, makes a man healthy, wealthy, and wise."
- "Well done is better than well said."

These phrases stuck with people because they were simple, direct, and useful. They weren't just random words—they were Franklin's beliefs about how to live a good and productive life.

The first edition of *Poor Richard's Almanack* was an immediate success. People loved it, not just for the weather predictions and calendars, but for the wit and wisdom it contained. Franklin kept writing new editions every year, and each one became more popular than the last. Over time, it became one of the best-selling publications in the American colonies.

Unlike many printers of the time, Franklin understood what made writing appealing to people. He didn't just print long, dull lists of facts—he made them interesting. He used humor, storytelling, and clever wordplay to keep readers entertained while also teaching them something useful. He wrote about hard work, honesty, thrift, and self-improvement, values he believed in deeply.

The success of *Poor Richard's Almanack* helped

Franklin's printing business grow. It brought in steady income, allowing him to expand and take on bigger projects. It also made him a well-known name, not just in Philadelphia but throughout the colonies. People quoted Poor Richard's sayings in their everyday conversations, passing them down through generations.

Franklin continued publishing the almanac for over twenty years. Even after he stopped, its influence remained strong. The sayings and advice from Poor Richard became part of American culture. Franklin had started it as a way to build his business, but it became much more than that. It was one of the ways he shaped the way people thought about work, success, and daily life.

5

BEN THE INVENTOR

Benjamin Franklin never stopped asking questions. He wasn't satisfied with knowing how things worked—he wanted to know why they worked. He wanted to test ideas, improve everyday life, and find new solutions to old problems. This curiosity led him to experiment constantly, even when there were no guarantees of success. He didn't just read about science—he put it into practice.

From an early age, he showed signs of being a natural problem solver. When he was a boy in Boston, he loved swimming, but he wasn't happy with how slow he moved through the water. Instead of just accepting it, he designed his own swim fins. Unlike the ones used today, his were made of wood and strapped to his hands. He tested them, adjusted them, and tried different ways to improve his speed. They weren't perfect, but they worked well enough to give him an advantage.

As he grew older, his experiments became more advanced. He was especially fascinated by electricity. At the time, people didn't fully understand what it was or how it worked. There were no light bulbs, no batteries, and no power lines—just strange sparks that scientists were trying to make sense of. Franklin wanted to learn everything he could about it. He studied the research of scientists in Europe and then conducted his own tests.

One of his most famous experiments involved lightning. He suspected that the sparks from electrical machines were similar to lightning bolts. To prove it, he flew a kite with a metal key attached to the string during a thunderstorm. When the key picked up an electrical charge, it showed that lightning was a form of electricity. This discovery helped lead to the invention of the lightning rod, a device that protected buildings from lightning strikes.

Franklin didn't just experiment with electricity. He also looked for ways to make everyday life better. He invented the Franklin stove, which produced more heat while using less wood. At a time when keeping warm in the winter was difficult, this was an important improvement. His stove design made homes more energy-efficient and was widely used for many years.

He also came up with the idea for bifocal glasses. As he got older, he found that he needed two different pairs of glasses—one for seeing things up close and another for seeing things far away. Instead of switching back and forth, he designed lenses that combined both prescriptions into a single pair of glasses. This simple idea made life easier for people with vision problems and is still used today.

Even his musical experiments led to new inventions. He created the glass armonica, a musical instrument that produced sound by rubbing wet fingers along spinning glass bowls. It became popular among musicians in Europe, and even famous composers like Mozart and Beethoven wrote music for it.

His love of experimenting extended beyond science and inventions. He was always looking for ways to improve how people lived and worked. He studied the effects of fresh air on health, tested theories about food and exercise, and even experimented with new ways to improve communication through the postal system.

The invention of the lightning rod

At the time, lightning was a serious problem. People feared storms, not just because of the thunder and rain, but because of the fires that often followed. Churches and tall buildings were especially vulnerable. A single lightning strike could set a wooden structure ablaze, destroying homes, barns, and even entire city blocks. There was no reliable way to stop these fires, and once they started, there was little anyone could do to save the buildings.

Franklin wanted to know if lightning could be guided safely away from buildings. He thought that if electricity in the lab could be attracted to metal, perhaps lightning could be as well. The question was how to test it. He came up with the idea of using a tall metal rod placed on top of a building, with a wire leading down to the ground. The rod, he theorized, would attract the lightning and direct the electrical charge harmlessly into the earth instead of allowing it to strike the structure itself.

Before putting his idea into practice, Franklin needed to confirm that lightning was indeed a form of electricity. He devised an experiment using a kite, a metal key, and a silk string. During a thunderstorm, he flew the kite with the key attached, holding onto the string through a dry silk ribbon to insulate himself. As the storm raged above, he noticed that the key began to spark when he brought his knuckle close to it. This proved his theory—lightning was electricity.

With this knowledge, he moved forward with his invention. He installed the first lightning rods on tall buildings in Philadelphia, including his own home. The rods were simple: a pointed metal pole stood at the highest point of the structure, connected to a wire that led safely into the ground. The idea was that when lightning struck, instead of hitting the building itself, it would be drawn to the rod and channeled harmlessly into the earth.

At first, not everyone accepted the idea. Some people believed that interfering with lightning was dangerous or even unnatural. But as more and more buildings equipped with lightning rods survived storms without catching fire, skepticism faded. Soon, the use of lightning rods spread beyond Philadelphia. Cities across the colonies, and even in Europe, began installing them to protect homes, churches, and public buildings.

Franklin's invention didn't just save buildings—it saved lives. Fires from lightning strikes became far less common, and communities that once lived in fear of thunderstorms now had a way to protect themselves. Scientists in Europe recognized Franklin's discovery as one of the most important breakthroughs in understanding electricity.

Unlike many inventors, Franklin didn't try to make money from the lightning rod. He believed that knowledge should be shared freely, especially when it had the potential to help so many people. His invention changed the way people thought about science, showing that curiosity and experimentation could lead to practical solutions for real-world problems.

Other inventions

One of his most famous inventions was bifocal glasses. As Franklin got older, he started having trouble with his vision. He needed one pair of glasses to see things up close and another pair to see things far away. Switching between two pairs was frustrating, and he knew there had to be a better way. He came up with the idea of combining the two prescriptions into a single lens. The top part of the lens helped him see things at a distance, while the bottom part was for reading or close work. Instead of carrying around multiple pairs of glasses, he could use just one.

Bifocals were a simple idea, but they made a huge difference. Once people saw how useful they were, others started using them too. Franklin wasn't the first person to experiment with different types of lenses, but he was the one who made bifocals popular. Today, millions of people wear them, and they still work the same way Franklin designed them.

Another one of his well-known inventions was the Franklin stove. During the 1700s, most people heated their homes with fireplaces. While fireplaces provided warmth, they weren't very efficient. A lot of the heat escaped through the chimney, which meant people had to burn a lot of wood just to keep their homes warm. This was a problem, especially in the winter when firewood was expensive and hard to find.

Franklin designed a better heating system. His stove was made of iron and used a special design that trapped more heat inside the room instead of letting it escape through the chimney. It used less wood but gave off more warmth. This made it a popular choice for homes, especially in colder areas. It also reduced the risk of fires, since it was safer than an open fireplace.

Unlike many inventors, Franklin didn't try to make money from his stove. He believed it was important for people to have access to useful inventions, so he didn't patent it. That meant other people could build and sell Franklin stoves without having to pay him. His goal wasn't to get rich—it was to help people stay warm while using fewer resources.

While Franklin was best known for his practical inventions, he also had a creative side. One of his more unusual inventions was the glass armonica, a musical instrument that produced sound by rubbing wet fingers along spinning glass bowls. Franklin had always been interested in music, and he wanted to create an instrument that had a soft, beautiful sound.

The armonica worked by using a series of glass bowls of different sizes, mounted on a spinning rod. When the musician touched the rims of the bowls with damp fingers, the friction created a sound similar to a singing voice. It was unlike any other instrument at the time. Famous composers like Mozart and Beethoven were fascinated by it and even wrote music for it.

Although the armonica never became as widely used as other instruments, it was admired for its unique and hauntingly beautiful sound. Even today, some musicians still play it, keeping Franklin's musical invention alive.

Each of Franklin's inventions showed his ability to solve problems and think differently. Whether it was improving vision, heating homes more efficiently, or creating a new way to make music, his ideas had a lasting impact. His curiosity and determination to make things better set him apart as not just an inventor, but a thinker who shaped everyday life in ways that are still felt today.

6

A SCIENTIST AND A THINKER

Electricity was a mystery in the 1700s. People knew it could produce sparks, make hair stand on end, and cause small shocks, but no one understood what caused it or how to control it. Franklin had been experimenting with ways to store electricity in devices called Leyden jars. These glass jars, coated with metal, could hold an electrical charge and release it in a single spark. He had seen how sparks could jump from metal to another object and wondered if the same thing happened in nature when lightning struck.

If he was right, it meant that electricity wasn't just something created in laboratories—it was part of the natural world. And if it was part of the natural world, maybe it could be controlled. Maybe people could find ways to protect buildings from lightning or even use electricity for practical purposes. But first, he needed to test his theory.

Franklin's idea was simple: if lightning was a form of electricity, it should behave the same way as the sparks he had been experimenting with. He needed a way to collect some of that lightning and test it. He thought about using a tall metal rod, but there was a problem—he had no way of safely reaching high enough to place one in a storm. Instead, he decided to use something he could send into the air: a kite.

To conduct the experiment, he built a simple kite using a wooden frame covered with a silk cloth. He attached a metal key to the string and made sure to hold onto the string with a dry silk ribbon to protect himself from getting shocked. He waited for a thunderstorm and then flew the kite into the sky, letting the wind carry it higher and higher.

As the storm passed over, Franklin noticed something remarkable. The metal key began to spark. When he brought his knuckle close to it, he felt a small shock—just like the shocks he had produced with his Leyden jars. This was the proof he had been looking for. Lightning and electricity were the same thing.

His experiment was a breakthrough. It showed that lightning wasn't a supernatural force or a mysterious event—it was a natural form of electricity that followed the same laws as the small electrical charges he had studied in his workshop. This discovery helped lead to one of his most important inventions, the lightning rod, which protected buildings from lightning strikes by safely directing the electrical charge into the ground.

Scientists in Europe were amazed by his experiment. His findings changed the way people thought about electricity and inspired more research into how it worked. Over time, Franklin's work helped pave the way for new discoveries about electrical energy, leading to inventions that would shape the modern world.

What he discovered about lightning

Benjamin Franklin had always been fascinated by electricity, but his kite experiment gave him something more than just proof that lightning and electricity were the same. It led him to new discoveries about how lightning worked, how it moved, and how it could be controlled. His findings didn't just change the way people understood storms—they led to practical inventions that made life safer.

Before Franklin's discoveries, people saw lightning as something mysterious and dangerous. It flashed across the sky, struck buildings, and often caused devastating fires. Many believed it was a sign from the heavens, something unpredictable and unstoppable. Franklin didn't accept that idea. He wanted to know exactly what lightning was and how it behaved.

One of the first things he realized was that lightning always tried to find the easiest path to the ground. It didn't just strike at random—it searched for the tallest objects and followed a direct route downward. This explained why churches and tall buildings were often the first to be hit during storms. It also helped him understand why trees were frequently struck. Their height made them natural targets, and when lightning hit, the electrical energy could split a tree in half or set it on fire instantly.

He also discovered that metal played a role in attracting and conducting electricity. The sparks he had observed in his workshop always moved toward metal objects, and he noticed the same thing happened during storms. This meant that lightning, like small electric sparks, could be directed. If it could be controlled, perhaps it could be prevented from causing harm.

Another important realization was that electricity didn't always behave in a straight line. He found that it could jump between objects, travel through the air, and follow unexpected paths. This was why some lightning strikes seemed to hit more than one place at a time. He saw that electrical charges built up in the clouds, and when the charge became strong enough, it discharged in a bolt of lightning.

His research also led him to understand the concept of grounding. If lightning was given a safe path to the ground, it wouldn't need to strike buildings or trees. This idea became the foundation for his most important invention, the lightning rod. By placing a pointed metal rod at the top of a building and connecting it to the ground with a wire, lightning could be directed safely away from structures.

Franklin's discoveries didn't just change the way people thought about lightning—they saved lives. Before his work, entire towns had been destroyed by lightning-caused fires. After his invention of the lightning rod, buildings were better protected, and the number of fires caused by storms dropped dramatically. Scientists across Europe and America recognized the importance of his research, and soon lightning rods were installed on homes, churches, and public buildings.

His work with electricity also led to further experiments by other scientists, eventually helping to develop new technologies. Understanding how lightning worked was the first step toward controlling electricity in useful ways. His discoveries paved the way for future scientists to continue exploring the nature of electrical energy, leading to the development of batteries, power grids, and modern electronics.

The impact of his scientific work

One of the biggest impacts of Franklin's work was in the field of electricity. His kite experiment wasn't just about proving that lightning was a form of electricity. It was one of the first demonstrations that electricity was a natural force that could be studied, measured, and controlled. Before Franklin, people thought of electricity as a mysterious phenomenon, something that appeared in flashes of lightning or the occasional sparks from rubbing objects together. His work helped shift the study of electricity from a curiosity into a real scientific discipline.

The lightning rod was one of the most practical results of his research. It saved lives and protected buildings across the world. Before lightning rods were common, a single lightning strike could set entire towns on fire. Tall buildings, particularly churches, were the most frequent targets. After Franklin's invention, cities installed lightning rods to redirect electrical charges safely into the ground. The design was simple but effective, and it's still used today.

Franklin's impact went beyond electricity. He was also one of the first people to chart the Gulf Stream, an ocean current that flows along the eastern coast of North America and across the Atlantic. Sailors had noticed that some routes across the ocean were faster than others, but they didn't understand why. Franklin studied ship logs, spoke with captains, and conducted tests to track the movement of warm and cold water. His maps of the Gulf Stream helped ships travel more efficiently, saving time and money.

He also contributed to the study of weather. He was one of the first scientists to suggest that storms moved in patterns instead of forming randomly. He observed that hurricanes and other major storms traveled from one place to another, rather than simply appearing and disappearing. His ideas helped lay the groundwork for modern meteorology, the science of studying the weather.

His experiments with heat and energy led to improvements in home heating. The Franklin stove, which he designed to use less wood while producing more heat, was an important advancement in home efficiency. At a time when staying warm in the winter required constant effort, his invention made heating homes safer and more effective.

His scientific work influenced people far beyond his lifetime. His discoveries helped inspire other scientists to explore electricity, leading to inventions like the battery and, later, the electrical power systems that run modern homes and cities. The simple idea that lightning and electricity were connected led to research that eventually made it possible to harness electrical energy for everyday use.

7

A LEADER IN THE COMMUNITY

In Philadelphia, books were rare. A few wealthy individuals owned private collections, but these were not open to the public. There were no public libraries like the ones that exist today. If someone wanted to learn about science, history, or philosophy, they had to either buy their own books or borrow from a friend. Franklin saw this as a problem. He knew that if people had access to books, they could educate themselves and improve their lives.

At the time, Franklin was part of a group of thinkers and writers called the Junto. The Junto was a club for men who wanted to discuss ideas, debate important topics, and share knowledge. The group met regularly to talk about politics, business, and science. Many of the members wanted to read more, but books were hard to come by. Franklin suggested a solution—what if they pooled their money and created a shared collection of books?

This idea led to the creation of the Library Company of Philadelphia in 1731. It was the first lending library in America. The members of the Junto contributed funds to purchase books, and they agreed that anyone who joined the library could borrow them. The idea was simple but powerful. Instead of each person struggling to build their own collection, they could share resources and give more people access to books.

The library's first collection included books on a wide range of topics. There were books on science, history, philosophy, and literature. Franklin made sure the selection included works that encouraged learning and critical thinking. The books were stored in a small room, and members could check them out for a certain period of time before returning them for others to read.

Word spread quickly. More people wanted access to the books, and the library grew. Eventually, it moved to a larger space and became an important center for learning in Philadelphia. Unlike the private collections owned by wealthy individuals, this library was designed for the community. Anyone who contributed could use it, regardless of their background or social status.

The success of Franklin's library inspired others to create similar institutions. Over time, lending libraries spread to other cities, making books more available to the public. What had started as a small idea among a group of friends became the foundation for the public library system.

Franklin's belief in education and knowledge didn't stop with the library. He later helped establish schools, newspapers, and scientific organizations. He knew that access to information could change lives, and he worked to create opportunities for people to learn and grow.

Founding the first volunteer fire department

Fire wasn't just a problem in Philadelphia. Cities in the 1700s didn't have the fire departments we have today. There were no full-time firefighters, no stations with fire engines, and no emergency numbers to call for help. If a fire broke out, people had to grab buckets of water and do their best to put it out. Often, it wasn't enough. Franklin knew something had to change.

. . .

He had seen how cities in Europe had organized fire brigades—groups of people who were trained and ready to respond when a fire broke out. He believed Philadelphia needed something similar. He started by writing about the issue in *The Pennsylvania Gazette*, warning people about the dangers of fire and urging them to take action. He didn't just want people to be aware of the problem—he wanted them to help solve it.

His efforts led to the creation of the Union Fire Company in 1736, the first volunteer fire department in the American colonies. It wasn't run by the government or a private company—it was made up of everyday people who agreed to work together to protect their city. They trained to respond quickly, used equipment more effectively, and created a system for stopping fires before they spread.

Each member of the fire company provided their own leather bucket, which was used to carry water. They also had ladders, hooks for pulling down burning buildings, and strong bags for rescuing valuable items from homes in danger. The group met regularly to practice, making sure they knew exactly what to do in an emergency.

OTHER FIRE COMPANIES FOLLOWED, and soon Philadelphia had a network of volunteer firefighters ready to respond when disaster struck. The idea spread to other cities, creating the foundation for modern fire departments. The system Franklin helped create made communities safer and saved countless lives.

FRANKLIN DIDN'T STOP AT JUST FORMING a fire department. He also encouraged fire prevention. He believed it was better to stop fires before they started rather than just fight them after they broke out. He wrote articles about how to build safer chimneys, store flammable materials properly, and keep houses free from fire hazards. He even promoted the idea of fire insurance, which helped people recover financially if their homes were damaged.

Improving postal service in the colonies

The mail system in the colonies was poorly managed. There were very few official post offices, and mail delivery was unreliable. Letters were sometimes carried by travelers who happened to be going in the right direction, but there was no organized system. In many cases, letters sat undelivered because no one was responsible for making sure they got where they needed to go. Franklin saw that a better postal system could help businesses grow, connect people, and strengthen the colonies.

In 1737, he was appointed postmaster of Philadelphia. This gave him control over the mail service in the city, and he immediately started making improvements. He organized delivery routes, hired reliable post riders, and made sure letters were sent out more efficiently. Under his leadership, Philadelphia's postal system became faster and more dependable.

His success in Philadelphia led to an even bigger opportunity. In 1753, he was made joint Postmaster General for all of the American colonies. This meant he was in charge of improving mail service across the entire region, from New England to the southern colonies. At the time, most letters between cities were delayed for weeks, sometimes lost along the way. Franklin wanted to fix that.

One of his first changes was creating better mail routes. He mapped out the fastest and most direct paths between major cities, cutting down travel times. He also made sure post riders carried mail on a regular schedule instead of waiting for enough letters to fill their bags. This simple change meant letters arrived more quickly and reliably.

Franklin also introduced milestones along roads to measure distances more accurately. This helped post riders know how far they had traveled and ensured they stayed on schedule. He inspected routes himself, sometimes riding on horseback for hundreds of miles to check on mail stations and see where improvements could be made.

Another major improvement was the creation of a night-riding mail system. Instead of stopping at sunset, some post riders continued through the night, allowing important messages to reach their destinations much faster. This was especially useful for government officials and businesses that depended on quick communication.

His work made the colonial postal service more efficient than ever before. Mail delivery times were cut in half, and more people began using the system.

Newspapers, which had often arrived too late to be useful, could now be delivered on time, keeping people informed about important news. Business owners were able to send and receive orders more quickly, helping the economy grow.

Franklin also made changes to how the postal service made money. Before his leadership, the postal system was losing money, but under his management, it started turning a profit. He made sure post offices collected proper fees, eliminated wasteful spending, and set up new post offices in growing towns.

His improvements had a lasting impact. The postal system he helped create became the foundation for the modern United States Postal Service. His ideas about efficiency, scheduled deliveries, and organized routes are still used today. Even after Franklin was removed from his position in 1774 for his growing support of American independence, the system he built remained strong.

8

FRANKLIN AND THE AMERICAN REVOLUTION

By the mid-1700s, life in the American colonies was changing. Towns were growing, businesses were thriving, and people were starting to see themselves as something different from the British subjects they had once been. They still considered themselves loyal to the British king, but they also saw that life in the colonies was not the same as life in England. They worked hard, built their own communities, and made their own decisions. But Britain still controlled them, and that control was becoming harder to accept.

The British government made the rules, but the people living in the colonies had little say in those decisions. Laws were passed in London, thousands of miles away, without input from the people they affected. Colonists had no representatives in the British Parliament, which meant they had no voice in how they were governed. This became a major issue as Britain started demanding more money from the colonies in the form of taxes.

The British government believed the colonies should help pay for the costs of running the empire, especially after the expensive French and Indian War. This war, which took place in North America between Britain and France, ended in 1763 with Britain winning control of more land. But the war had cost Britain a great deal of money. To recover those costs, the British government turned to the American colonies. They passed new taxes, expecting the colonists to pay their share.

The problem wasn't just the taxes themselves—it was the fact that the colonists had no choice in the matter. They were being taxed without having any representatives in Parliament to argue on their behalf. This led to the famous phrase: **"No taxation without representation."** The colonists believed that if they were going to be taxed, they should have a say in how the money was used.

One of the first major taxes was the **Stamp Act of 1765.** This law required colonists to pay for an official stamp on printed materials, including newspapers, playing cards, and legal documents. People were outraged. Newspapers wrote angry articles, protests broke out, and some people even refused to buy British goods. The protests worked—the British government eventually repealed the Stamp Act. But they soon passed new taxes, leading to more anger.

The **Townshend Acts** of 1767 placed taxes on everyday goods like glass, paint, and tea. Many colonists responded by boycotting British products, refusing to buy them as a way to protest the unfair laws. Once again, Britain backed down on most of the taxes, but they kept one—the tax on tea. This led to one of the most famous acts of protest in American history: the **Boston Tea Party** of 1773.

A group of colonists, angry about the continued tax on tea, disguised themselves and boarded British ships in Boston Harbor. They dumped 342 chests of tea into the water to send a message to the British government. This act of defiance only made Britain more determined to control the colonies. They passed harsh laws, known as the **Intolerable Acts**, to punish Boston. The British closed the harbor, placed Massachusetts under strict British rule, and ordered colonists to house British soldiers in their homes.

By this time, many colonists were starting to

believe that Britain would never treat them fairly. They saw their rights being ignored and their voices being silenced. Groups like the **Sons of Liberty** encouraged resistance, and colonial leaders began meeting to discuss what could be done.

Benjamin Franklin had watched these events unfold. He had spent much of his life working to strengthen the colonies, improve communication, and make life better for people. He had always been loyal to Britain, but even he began to see that the British government was not treating the colonies with fairness or respect. Franklin had spent years in London as a representative for Pennsylvania, trying to convince British leaders to listen to colonial concerns. But he saw firsthand that Britain was unwilling to compromise.

More and more colonists began to believe that they could no longer be ruled by Britain. They wanted to govern themselves, make their own laws, and control their own future. This idea was growing stronger, and soon, it would lead to a movement for independence. Franklin, once a loyal British subject, would find himself at the center of that fight.

His role in the Declaration of Independence

By 1776, it was clear that the colonies and Britain could no longer find a way to work together. Years of unfair taxes, harsh laws, and government control had led many people to believe that the only solution was independence. The colonies had tried sending petitions and representatives to Britain, hoping to convince the king to treat them fairly. But Britain refused to listen. Instead, British soldiers were sent to put down any protests, and the situation grew more dangerous.

Many colonial leaders realized they needed to take a bold step—breaking away from Britain completely. It was not an easy decision. Britain was the most powerful empire in the world, and the colonies had no real army, no government of their own, and no guarantee that they would survive on their own. If they failed, the leaders who supported independence could be executed for treason. It was a risk, but they believed that freedom was worth it.

Benjamin Franklin had spent much of his life believing in cooperation. He had worked to improve the colonies, strengthen their connection to Britain, and encourage peaceful solutions. But after years of seeing Britain ignore colonial concerns, he knew independence was the only way forward. He had been in London representing Pennsylvania when the crisis grew worse, and he had witnessed firsthand how little British leaders cared about the colonies. By the time he returned to America, he was fully in favor of breaking away from British rule.

In the spring of 1776, the colonies sent representatives to the **Second Continental Congress** in Philadelphia. This meeting brought together some of the most important leaders of the time, including Thomas Jefferson, John Adams, and Benjamin Franklin. They debated what to do next. Some still hoped for peace, but most agreed that the time had come for independence. A committee was formed to write a document that would explain to the world why the colonies were declaring themselves free from Britain.

Franklin was chosen to be part of this **Committee of Five**, the group responsible for writing what would become the **Declaration of Independence**. Along with Franklin, the committee included **Thomas Jefferson, John Adams, Roger Sherman, and Robert Livingston**. They had to put into words the reasons why the colonies were separating from Britain and what kind of government they hoped to build.

Thomas Jefferson was chosen to write the first draft. He was a strong writer and had already expressed his ideas about freedom and government in previous writings. While Jefferson worked on the draft, Franklin and the others gave advice and made suggestions. Franklin, known for his careful use of words and diplomatic style, helped refine the document, making sure it was clear, strong, and persuasive.

One of Franklin's most famous contributions was a small but important change in wording. In Jefferson's original draft, there was a line that said, **"We hold these truths to be sacred and undeniable."** Franklin suggested changing it to **"We hold these truths to be self-evident."** This change made the statement more powerful, emphasizing that the right to freedom wasn't based on religious belief, but on reason and human rights.

When the final draft was presented to the Continental Congress on **July 2, 1776**, the delegates debated it for two days. Some parts were removed, others were edited, but the core message remained the same: the colonies were declaring themselves free from Britain. Franklin supported the document completely, knowing it was a turning point in history.

On **July 4, 1776,** the Declaration of Independence was officially adopted. Franklin, along with the other leaders, signed it. He understood what this meant—it was a direct challenge to the British king. Anyone who signed the document was putting their life on the line. If the revolution failed, they would be seen as traitors. Franklin is said to have made a famous remark at the signing:

"We must all hang together, or, most assuredly, we shall all hang separately."

He meant that the colonies had to stand united. If they didn't support each other, they would be defeated, and every one of them would face punishment from Britain. But Franklin also knew that their cause was just. He had spent years studying government, history, and human rights, and he believed that people had the right to govern themselves.

The Declaration of Independence was sent to Britain and other countries, announcing to the world that the thirteen American colonies were now a free and independent nation. The war for independence was far from over, but the signing of the document was a defining moment. Franklin's role in shaping and supporting the Declaration helped set the foundation for the new United States.

Traveling to France to ask for help

Winning independence from Britain was not going to be easy. The American colonies had declared themselves free, but they were up against the most powerful military in the world. Britain had warships, trained soldiers, and money to fund a long war. The colonies had farmers and shopkeepers fighting as soldiers, few supplies, and almost no money. If they were going to have a real chance at victory, they needed help.

Benjamin Franklin understood this better than most. He had spent years in London before the war, trying to negotiate with British leaders. He knew how strong the British Empire was, and he knew that the colonies couldn't win without support from other countries. France was Britain's biggest rival, and Franklin believed the French might be willing to help. If France sent money, supplies, and soldiers, the American army would have a much better chance of defeating Britain.

In 1776, Franklin was chosen to travel to France to convince the French government to become an ally of the United States. At seventy years old, he was no longer a young man, but he was one of the most respected and well-known Americans. His writings, scientific discoveries, and political experience made him the perfect choice for the job.

The journey across the Atlantic was dangerous. The British Navy patrolled the waters, looking for American ships. If Franklin's ship had been captured, he could have been arrested and sent back to Britain as a traitor. But he arrived safely in France in December 1776 and immediately began working to win support for the American cause.

France had a long history of fighting with Britain. The two nations had been enemies for centuries, and France had lost land to Britain in the French and Indian War. Many French leaders wanted to weaken Britain, but they weren't sure whether the American colonies could actually win the war. France didn't want to send money and soldiers to fight against Britain unless they believed the Americans had a real chance. Franklin's job was to convince them that the colonies were strong enough to win, but only if they had France's help.

He became a celebrity in France. People admired his intelligence and charm, and they were fascinated by his simple way of dressing. Unlike many wealthy European politicians, Franklin didn't wear fancy wigs or elaborate clothes. He dressed in plain suits and carried himself like an ordinary man. This made him even more popular, and many French citizens supported the idea of helping the American colonies.

Franklin met with French officials, including King Louis XVI and his advisers. He explained why the American colonies wanted independence and why France should support them. He used his skills as a writer and speaker to persuade them that helping the United States would not only weaken Britain but also create a powerful new trade partner for France.

At first, France hesitated. They wanted proof that the Americans could stand up to Britain in battle. That proof came in 1777 when the American army won a major victory at the **Battle of Saratoga**. This showed France that the American colonies had a real chance of winning the war. After that, Franklin worked even harder to secure an alliance.

In 1778, France officially agreed to help the United States. This was a turning point in the war. France sent money, soldiers, and ships to fight against Britain. Without this support, the American colonies might not have won their independence. Franklin's work as a diplomat had paid off.

9

THE WISE OLD STATESMAN

After the American Revolution, the states had their own governments, but there was no single system that connected them in a clear and effective way. The original plan for government, known as the **Articles of Confederation**, was weak. Congress had little power to enforce laws, raise money, or settle disputes between states. Each state acted almost like its own independent country, and this caused many problems. Leaders across the country knew something had to change. They needed a new system—one that would keep the states united while still protecting individual freedoms.

A meeting was called in Philadelphia to fix these problems. It became known as the **Constitutional**

Convention, and Franklin was chosen as one of the delegates from Pennsylvania. Even though he was much older than most of the other delegates, his experience and wisdom made him one of the most respected people in the room. He had spent years studying governments, debating ideas, and thinking about the best way to create a fair system. People listened when he spoke, and his ability to compromise made him an important voice in the discussion.

The convention wasn't easy. The delegates had strong opinions about how the new government should work, and they often argued. Some wanted a strong central government, while others wanted the states to keep most of the power. Some believed larger states should have more influence, while smaller states worried they would be ignored. There were also major disagreements over slavery and how it would be addressed in the new government. The debates went on for months, and at times, it seemed like the delegates would never agree.

Franklin didn't speak often, but when he did, his words carried weight. He knew that the future of the country depended on compromise. He urged the delegates to set aside their differences and focus on what was best for the nation as a whole. He reminded them that no system of government would be perfect, but they had an opportunity to create something better than anything that had come before.

One of Franklin's most important contributions was his call for unity. He understood that if the states did not come together under a strong constitution, the new nation could fall apart. He famously told the delegates, **"We must, indeed, all hang together, or, most assuredly, we shall all hang separately."** This was the same idea he had shared during the Revolution—if the states didn't work together, they would fail on their own.

After months of debate, the delegates finally created the **United States Constitution**, a document that would become the foundation of American government. It established three branches—**the executive (president), the legislative (Congress), and the judicial (courts)**—to balance power and prevent any one part of the government from becoming too strong. It also included a system of checks and balances, ensuring that each branch had the ability to keep the others from abusing their power.

His role at the Constitutional Convention

By the time the Constitutional Convention began in May 1787, Benjamin Franklin was 81 years old. He was the oldest delegate in the room, and many of the younger men looked up to him as a wise leader. His body was weak—he often had to be carried in a special chair—but his mind was still sharp. He had spent a lifetime thinking about government, freedom, and how to build a strong society. Now, he had one more important job to do: help create a government that would last.

The convention was held in **Philadelphia**, the city Franklin had helped shape. The delegates from the 13 states gathered in the **Pennsylvania State House** (now known as Independence Hall) to solve the problems caused by the **Articles of Confederation**, the first attempt at a government. The Articles had made the national government too weak. Congress had little power, and the states acted almost like separate countries. There were arguments over trade, money, and even laws. Franklin and the other delegates knew that if something wasn't done, the country might fall apart.

The meetings were long and difficult. There was no air conditioning, and the hot summer air made tempers rise along with the temperature inside the hall. The delegates debated for months over big issues, such as how much power the national government should have, how states should be represented, and whether slavery should be allowed. Arguments broke out often, and at times, it seemed like the delegates would never agree.

Franklin did not speak as often as others, but when he did, people listened. He understood that the success of the convention depended on **compromise**. Some delegates wanted a strong central government, while others wanted the states to keep most of their power. Large states wanted more representation in Congress, while smaller states worried about being ignored. Franklin's job was to encourage unity and remind the delegates that they were building something bigger than themselves.

One of the biggest debates was over how states would be represented in Congress. The larger states wanted representation based on population, while the smaller states wanted each state to have an equal vote. This argument nearly tore the convention apart. Franklin supported what became known as the **Great Compromise**, which created a two-part Congress: the **House of Representatives**, where representation was based on population, and the

Senate, where each state had two senators, no matter its size. This idea helped bring the states together, giving both sides something they could accept.

Franklin also played a key role in **promoting cooperation.** He knew that the delegates came from different backgrounds and had different interests, but they needed to work together for the good of the country. At one point, when arguments had gone on for weeks without progress, Franklin stood and gave a powerful speech. He suggested that the delegates begin each day with a prayer, asking for guidance in their decision-making. While the idea of starting with prayer wasn't adopted, Franklin's speech reminded everyone that their mission was bigger than their personal disagreements.

Another issue that caused serious debate was slavery. Some delegates wanted to ban it completely, while others refused to support a Constitution that threatened slavery in the Southern states. Franklin, who had once owned enslaved people but later became a strong **abolitionist,** hoped to end slavery. However, he knew that the convention would fall apart if the delegates could not agree. Instead, compromises were made, leaving the issue of slavery unresolved—a decision that would lead to major conflicts in the future.

By **September 1787**, after months of difficult debates, the delegates finally agreed on a final draft of the **United States Constitution**. Franklin was too weak to stand and read a speech himself, so another delegate read his final remarks. He admitted that no government was perfect, but he believed that this Constitution was the best possible plan. He urged every delegate to put aside their doubts and sign it.

His beliefs about freedom and democracy

Benjamin Franklin spent his life thinking about what makes a good government. He had lived under British rule, fought for American independence, and helped create a new government from the ground up. He had seen what happened when leaders had too much power and how unfair laws could harm ordinary people. By the time he helped write the U.S. Constitution, he had strong ideas about freedom, democracy, and the responsibilities of a government.

One of Franklin's most important beliefs was that a government should serve the people, not the other way around. He had seen how the British government ignored the concerns of the American colonists. The king and Parliament passed laws and taxes without asking for input from the people who had to follow them. Franklin believed that a fair government needed to represent the people's interests, not just the wishes of a small group of rulers. This idea was central to democracy—the belief that people should have a say in how they are governed.

Franklin also believed that freedom wasn't just something people were given—it was something they had to work to protect. He knew that even a well-designed government could become unfair if people didn't stay involved. He warned that freedom could disappear if people didn't pay attention to what their leaders were doing. After the Constitutional Convention, when someone asked Franklin what kind of government the delegates had created, he famously responded, **"A republic, if you can keep it."** He meant that democracy could only survive if people took responsibility for making sure their leaders stayed fair and honest.

He also believed that education was essential for a strong democracy. He thought that people needed to understand their rights and responsibilities in order to make good decisions. This is one reason he

Lightning, Libraries, and Liberty

helped start the first public lending library—he wanted more people to have access to knowledge. He believed that an informed public could prevent corrupt leaders from taking too much power.

Franklin was a strong supporter of free speech and freedom of the press. He had been a printer for most of his life, and he understood the power of words. He believed that people should be able to express their opinions openly, even if those opinions were unpopular. He thought newspapers and books played a big role in keeping people informed and making sure the government stayed accountable.

Another belief Franklin held was that democracy worked best when people worked together for the common good. He spent much of his life organizing groups that improved communities, like the first volunteer fire department and the first public hospital in America. He believed that individuals had a responsibility to help their neighbors and that a strong society depended on people looking out for one another.

His views on equality also shaped his ideas about government. He had once owned enslaved people, but as he grew older, he realized that slavery was wrong. He became a leader in the fight to end slavery and worked with abolitionist groups to push for change. He believed that freedom should belong to everyone, not just a select group of people.

10

THE LEGACY OF BENJAMIN FRANKLIN

Benjamin Franklin died in 1790, but the things he created and the ideas he believed in are still shaping the world today. He wasn't just a man of his time—he was a thinker, an inventor, and a leader whose influence can still be seen in modern life. Many of the things he worked on, from science to government, continue to affect how people live, learn, and communicate.

One of the most obvious ways Franklin's work still matters is in **electricity.** He didn't invent electricity, but his experiments helped people understand it better. His famous kite experiment proved that lightning was a form of electricity, which led to the invention of the **lightning rod.** Today, lightning rods are still used on buildings to protect them from dangerous lightning strikes. His research into electricity helped inspire scientists who later created batteries, power plants, and the electrical systems that power homes, schools, and businesses.

His **bifocal glasses** continue to help people see clearly. Many people today have the same problem Franklin had—difficulty seeing things both up close and far away. His invention of combining two different lenses into one pair of glasses is still used in bifocals, making it easier for millions of people to read, drive, and do everyday tasks without switching between different pairs of glasses.

The **Franklin stove** was an important invention in home heating. Before Franklin's design, fireplaces wasted a lot of heat and required large amounts of wood. His stove was more efficient, keeping homes warmer while using less fuel. While modern heating systems have advanced far beyond wood-burning stoves, the idea of **energy efficiency** that Franklin promoted is still an important part of modern inventions. Many of today's heating and cooling systems are designed with the same goal—using less energy while providing more warmth or cooling.

Franklin also left a lasting impact on **communication**. As a printer, writer, and newspaper publisher, he understood the importance of sharing information. He helped improve the postal system in the colonies, making mail delivery faster and more reliable. His work eventually led to the creation of what is now the **United States Postal Service**, which still delivers mail across the country. His belief in **free speech and freedom of the press** helped shape the First Amendment to the U.S. Constitution, protecting people's right to express their opinions.

One of his biggest contributions was in **education and libraries**. He believed that knowledge should be available to everyone, not just the wealthy. He helped create the first **public lending library**, an idea that led to the public libraries we have today. His belief that education was essential for a strong democracy influenced the creation of schools, universities, and institutions dedicated to lifelong learning. Many of the things he valued—reading, curiosity, and self-improvement—are still encouraged in schools and libraries around the world.

His contributions to **government and democracy** are some of his most lasting achievements. He helped write the **Declaration of Independence** and the **U.S. Constitution**, shaping the principles of the American government. The idea that people should have a say in their government, that power should be balanced among different branches, and that individual rights should be protected—all of these ideas were supported by Franklin and are still central to American democracy today. His famous warning, **"A republic, if you can keep it,"** is a reminder that democracy depends on people staying involved, voting, and paying attention to what their leaders are doing.

Franklin also influenced **science and medicine**. He helped establish the first public hospital in America, recognizing that healthcare should be available to everyone. He studied the spread of disease and promoted ideas about cleanliness and public health that are still followed today. His curiosity about how things worked—whether it was electricity, heat, or even the ocean's **Gulf Stream**—led to discoveries that scientists built upon for years.

His ideas about **community service and civic duty** continue to inspire people. Franklin didn't just work for himself; he worked to make life better for others. He founded the first volunteer fire department, encouraged people to work together to solve problems, and believed that strong communities were built through cooperation. Today, volunteer organizations, charities, and civic groups still follow his example by helping those in need and improving neighborhoods.

Famous quotes and life lessons from Ben Franklin

Benjamin Franklin was full of ideas, but he was also full of wisdom. He didn't just invent things or help create a country—he also thought deeply about how people should live. He believed in hard work, curiosity, and kindness, and he shared his thoughts through writing. Many of his sayings from **Poor Richard's Almanack** and his other writings are still repeated today. His words have lasted because they offer practical advice about life, success, and character.

One of his most well-known quotes is **"An investment in knowledge pays the best interest."** Franklin believed that learning was one of the best things a person could do. He saw education as a way for people to improve themselves and their communities. He had very little formal schooling as a child, but he never stopped reading and studying. He built libraries, wrote books, and encouraged others to learn as much as they could. His words remind people that knowledge is something valuable that never loses its worth.

Another famous saying is **"Well done is better than well said."** Franklin understood that talk alone wasn't enough—action was what truly mattered. He saw many people who made big promises but never followed through. To him, proving yourself through your actions was more important than simply saying the right things. Whether someone is working on a project, practicing a skill, or trying to be a better person, this quote is a reminder that effort and results are more important than just good intentions.

One of his most quoted pieces of advice is **"Early to bed and early to rise makes a man healthy, wealthy, and wise."** Franklin believed in having a good routine. He followed a daily schedule that included time for work, learning, and reflection. He understood that good habits could lead to success, and he encouraged people to take care of themselves, use their time wisely, and work toward their goals. Even today, many people try to follow similar routines, knowing that structure and discipline can make a big difference in life.

Franklin also valued money and financial responsibility. One of his most famous sayings is **"A penny saved is a penny earned."** He believed that being careful with money was just as important as earning it. He encouraged people to save and avoid wasteful spending. This advice is still relevant today, especially for people who want to manage their money wisely. Even though the value of a penny has changed since Franklin's time, the lesson remains the same—small savings add up over time.

His thoughts on personal responsibility and self-improvement are reflected in his quote, **"Do not squander time, for that's the stuff life is made of."** Franklin was always thinking about how to make the most of each day. He knew that time, once lost, could never be regained. He encouraged people to stay productive, set goals, and avoid wasting their hours on things that didn't matter. He believed that every moment was an opportunity to learn, grow, and contribute something meaningful.

One of his strongest beliefs was in honesty and character. He once wrote, **"Honesty is the best policy."** Franklin understood that being truthful was important in both business and personal life. He believed that people who were honest gained respect and trust, while those who were dishonest often found themselves in trouble. He lived by this idea, building a reputation for being fair, wise, and trustworthy.

Franklin also believed in the power of kindness and generosity. He said, **"When you are good to others, you are best to yourself."** He encouraged people to help their neighbors, support their communities, and share knowledge. His own life reflected this—he never patented his inventions because he wanted people to be able to use them freely. He believed that improving the world around him was more important than personal gain.

His words also remind people that small actions can lead to big changes. **"Little strokes fell great oaks."** This saying means that even the biggest challenges can be overcome if tackled one step at a time. Franklin knew that hard work and persistence could lead to success. Whether writing a book, learning a new skill, or working toward a goal, steady effort over time makes a difference.

His belief in unity and teamwork is reflected in his quote, **"We must all hang together, or, most assuredly, we shall all hang separately."** Franklin said this during the signing of the Declaration of Independence, reminding his fellow revolutionaries that they needed to stay united. He understood that people accomplish more when they work together, whether in government, business, or everyday life. His words are still used today to encourage cooperation and teamwork.

CONCLUSION

Benjamin Franklin never stopped asking questions. He wanted to know how the world worked, why things happened, and what could be done to make life better. He didn't just accept things as they were—he explored, experimented, and searched for answers. This curiosity led him to become a scientist, an inventor, a writer, and a leader. His life shows that curiosity isn't just about learning facts—it's about thinking deeply, making discoveries, and solving problems.

He didn't wait for someone to teach him. As a boy, he had little formal schooling, but that didn't stop him from learning. He taught himself by reading, asking questions, and trying new things. When he wanted to become a better writer, he studied great works of writing and practiced. When he was interested in electricity, he performed experiments. When he saw a problem in his community, he worked on a solution. Franklin's life proves that curiosity isn't enough on its own—it must be combined with effort.

Hard work was at the center of everything Franklin did. He believed that success didn't come from luck but from effort and persistence. He started working at a young age, first in his brother's print shop and later in his own business. He built a successful printing company, but he didn't stop there. He used his time wisely, waking up early and following a daily schedule. He believed that small, consistent actions could lead to big results.

He didn't let failure stop him. Throughout his life, he faced challenges, disagreements, and setbacks. He struggled in business, had ideas rejected, and even lost jobs. But instead of giving up, he adjusted, learned from his mistakes, and kept moving forward. His belief in hard work and perseverance helped him become one of the most respected figures in history.

Franklin also believed in self-improvement. He made a list of virtues he wanted to follow, including honesty, humility, and discipline. He didn't expect perfection, but he worked every day to become better. He understood that learning and growing never stop. His focus on improving himself also made him determined to improve the world around him.

He looked for ways to help others. He didn't just think about himself—he wanted to make his community stronger. He helped create libraries so more people could read and learn. He started a fire department to keep his city safe. He improved the postal system so people could communicate better. His ideas helped not just individuals but entire communities.

Franklin's life is a reminder that curiosity and hard work can lead to great things. He showed that asking questions, exploring new ideas, and putting in effort can open doors to knowledge and success. His belief in lifelong learning, self-discipline, and helping others are lessons that remain valuable today. His story proves that no matter where a person starts, curiosity and determination can make a lasting impact.

How we can be problem solvers like Ben

Benjamin Franklin didn't just accept things the way they were—he looked for ways to make them better. He saw problems as challenges to solve, not just obstacles to complain about. Whether it was figuring out how to protect buildings from lightning, improving mail delivery, or helping create a better government, he found solutions by thinking carefully, experimenting, and working with others. His approach to problem-solving can still be used today, no matter the challenge.

One of the first things Franklin did when facing a problem was **ask questions.** He didn't assume he knew everything. Instead, he looked at a situation and wondered how it could be improved. When he was young and struggling to write well, he didn't give up. He asked himself, "What makes a piece of writing good? How do great writers organize their thoughts?" Then he studied their work, took notes, and practiced. He didn't wait for someone to fix the problem for him—he took the first step.

He also believed in **testing ideas.** If something didn't work the first time, he didn't see it as failure. He saw it as an opportunity to learn. When he was experimenting with electricity, he didn't stop at one test. He tried different methods to understand how electricity moved and how it could be controlled. His famous kite experiment helped prove that lightning was a form of electricity, leading to the invention of the lightning rod. He knew that mistakes weren't the end of a process—they were part of the process.

Franklin didn't just think about **his own problems**—he looked for ways to help others. When he noticed that books were expensive and hard to find, he helped create the first lending library. When he saw that fires were a danger to Philadelphia, he helped organize the first volunteer fire department. When he realized that letters took too long to be delivered, he worked on improving the postal system. He didn't just come up with ideas—he worked to turn them into real solutions that benefited entire communities.

He also understood that **small improvements add up over time.** He believed that people could always improve themselves and their surroundings if they put in steady effort. He once said, **"Little strokes fell great oaks,"** meaning that even the biggest challenges could be solved by working on them bit by bit. This idea applies to all kinds of problems, whether learning a new skill, improving a habit, or fixing something in a community.

Franklin's problem-solving didn't just come from books—it came from **observing the world.** He paid attention to how things worked and noticed patterns. His studies of the ocean's **Gulf Stream** helped sailors understand how currents affected travel. His experiments with **heat and air movement** led to the Franklin stove, which made homes warmer while using less fuel. He believed that paying attention to details could lead to big discoveries.

Another key part of Franklin's approach was **working with others.** He knew that problems were often too big to solve alone. Whether he was helping draft the Declaration of Independence or working with scientists on experiments, he listened to different ideas and worked as part of a team. He didn't just focus on what he wanted—he looked for solutions that worked for everyone.

One of Franklin's greatest strengths was his **ability to adapt.** If something didn't go as planned, he adjusted and tried a new approach. He understood that problems didn't always have one simple answer. When arguments broke out at the Constitutional Convention, he didn't demand that everyone agree with him. Instead, he encouraged **compro-**

mise, helping create a government system that balanced different views.

His life is proof that problem-solving is about more than just being smart—it's about being curious, determined, and willing to try different solutions. He didn't solve problems by waiting for someone else to fix things. He asked questions, experimented, observed, worked with others, and kept going even when things were difficult.

Being a problem solver like Franklin doesn't mean inventing a new machine or writing a famous document. It can mean looking for small ways to improve daily life, thinking creatively about challenges, and never stopping the search for solutions. His example shows that no matter how big or small a problem is, a curious mind and hard work can make a difference.

A TIMELINE OF FRANKLIN'S LIFE
1706 – A FUTURE THINKER IS BORN

Benjamin Franklin was born on **January 17, 1706**, in **Boston, Massachusetts**. He was the 15th of 17 children in his family, which meant life was busy and often crowded. His father, Josiah Franklin, made soap and candles, while his mother, Abiah Folger, managed the household. From an early age, Franklin showed curiosity about the world, and even though he had little formal schooling, he found ways to learn on his own.

1718 – Learning the Printing Trade

At just **12 years old**, Franklin became an apprentice to his older brother James, who ran a printing business. This job introduced him to books, newspapers, and the power of the written word. He didn't always get along with his brother, but he learned

1722 – Writing Under a Secret Name

While working at the printing shop, Franklin wanted to publish his own ideas, but he knew his brother wouldn't allow it. He came up with a clever plan—he wrote letters using the fake name **Silence Dogood**, pretending to be a middle-aged widow. These letters were published in his brother's newspaper, and readers loved them. When Franklin revealed he was the true author, it caused trouble with his brother, leading to more arguments between them.

1723 – Running Away to Philadelphia

By the age of 17, Franklin had enough of his brother's strict rules and decided to leave Boston. He made his way to **Philadelphia**, arriving with almost no money. Despite having little, he found work as a printer and began building a new life in the city that would later become his home.

1724 – A Journey to England

Franklin traveled to **London, England**, expecting to find a great opportunity, but instead, he struggled to find steady work. Even though his plans didn't work out as he had hoped, he used his time there to learn more about printing and expand his knowledge. When he returned to Philadelphia two years later, he was ready to start his own business.

1729 – The Pennsylvania Gazette

Franklin became the owner of a newspaper, **The Pennsylvania Gazette**, which became one of the most popular newspapers in the American colonies. He used it to share news, opinions, and ideas that encouraged discussion and learning.

1733 – Poor Richard's Almanack

Franklin published the first edition of **Poor Richard's Almanack**, a book filled with weather predictions, advice, and wise sayings. It became incredibly popular and was published every year for 25 years. Many of his famous quotes, like **"A penny saved is a penny earned"**, came from this almanac.

1736 – Starting the First Volunteer Fire Department

Fires were a huge problem in Philadelphia, and Franklin saw the need for a better way to fight them. He helped create the **Union Fire Company**, the first volunteer fire department in America. His idea of neighbors helping each other in emergencies is still the foundation of fire departments today.

1743 – Founding the American Philosophical Society

Franklin loved discussing ideas with other

thinkers, so he started the **American Philosophical Society,** a group where scientists and inventors could share discoveries and inventions. This society still exists today, supporting learning and exploration.

1749 – Helping Create the First Public Library and College

Believing that education should be available to everyone, Franklin helped create the **Library Company of Philadelphia,** which allowed people to borrow books. He also helped establish what later became the **University of Pennsylvania,** a school that encouraged practical learning.

1752 – The Kite Experiment and Electricity

Franklin wanted to prove that lightning was a form of electricity, so he conducted his famous **kite experiment.** He flew a kite with a key attached during a storm, and when the key attracted an electric charge, he showed that lightning was indeed electrical. This discovery led to the invention of the **lightning rod,** which protected buildings from lightning strikes.

1754 – The Albany Plan of Union

Franklin believed the American colonies should work together, and he proposed the **Albany Plan of Union,** an idea for a united government. While it wasn't adopted at the time, it was an early step toward the idea of a United States.

1757 – Traveling to England as a Diplomat

Franklin spent many years in **London**, representing Pennsylvania and later all the colonies. He tried to convince British leaders to treat the colonies fairly, but he realized that Britain wasn't willing to give the colonies more freedom.

1775 – The Start of the American Revolution

As tensions grew between Britain and the colonies, Franklin supported the fight for independence. He was part of the **Second Continental Congress**, where leaders debated breaking away from Britain.

1776 – Signing the Declaration of Independence

Franklin helped draft and signed the **Declaration of Independence**, making the United States a new nation. He famously said, **"We must all hang together, or, most assuredly, we shall all hang separately,"** reminding the other leaders that unity was important.

1776 – Traveling to France for Support

Franklin went to **France** to convince the French government to help the United States in the war against Britain. He used his charm, intelligence, and diplomacy to win France's support, which became a turning point in the war.

1783 – The End of the War

After years of fighting, the war ended with the **Treaty of Paris**, which Franklin helped negotiate. Britain officially recognized the United States as an independent country.

1787 – Helping Write the U.S. Constitution

Franklin played a key role at the **Constitutional Convention**, where leaders designed the new government. Even though he was 81 years old, he encouraged cooperation and compromise to create a strong, lasting democracy.

1790 – Franklin's Final Years

Franklin spent his last years continuing to write, support education, and fight against **slavery**. He passed away on **April 17, 1790**, at the age of 84. His funeral was attended by thousands, showing how much people respected his contributions.

ACTIVITIES

Benjamin Franklin was always curious about the world around him. He asked questions, tested ideas, and experimented to find answers. One of his most famous scientific discoveries was about electricity. He wanted to understand how lightning worked and whether it was connected to electricity, so he conducted his famous kite experiment. Today, scientists have much safer ways to study electricity, but Franklin's curiosity about static electricity and electrical charges can still be explored through simple experiments.

One easy way to explore static electricity, just like Franklin did, is with a **Balloon & Static Electricity Experiment.** This experiment demonstrates how static electricity builds up and how it can attract or repel objects. It doesn't require any special equipment, and it's a great way to see one of Franklin's discoveries in action.

What You'll Need:

- One or two balloons
- A wool sweater, a clean cloth, or your hair
- Small pieces of paper (cut into tiny bits)
- A metal spoon
- A running faucet (optional for extra exploration)

Step 1: Creating Static Electricity

Start by blowing up a balloon and tying it closed. Hold the balloon firmly and rub it against a wool sweater, a dry cloth, or even your hair. Rub it back and forth quickly for about 10 to 15 seconds. This rubbing action creates **static electricity**, which means you are transferring tiny electrical charges to the surface of the balloon.

Franklin didn't have balloons when he studied electricity, but he noticed that certain materials could hold an electrical charge. He experimented with glass, metal, and even his own body to understand how electrical charges moved.

Step 2: Attracting Small Objects

Place the tiny pieces of paper on a table or flat surface. Slowly bring the charged balloon near the paper. Watch what happens! The pieces of paper should **jump up and stick to the balloon.** This happens because the paper is attracted to the static charge on the balloon.

Franklin was one of the first scientists to study **how objects could attract or repel each other due to electricity.** He discovered that objects could have **positive and negative charges**, which create the force that pulls things together or pushes them apart.

Step 3: Repelling Objects

Now, take a second balloon and repeat the same rubbing process to create static electricity on both balloons. Hold the two charged balloons close to each other. This time, instead of pulling together, the balloons should **push away from each other.**

This happens because both balloons have the same type of electrical charge, and charges that are the same **repel** each other. Franklin studied this same effect when he experimented with different objects, learning that opposite charges attract, while similar charges push apart.

Step 4: Bending Water (Optional Experiment)

If you want to take this experiment further, turn

on a faucet and let a thin stream of water flow. Take the charged balloon and bring it close to the stream of water **without touching it.** The water should bend toward the balloon!

This happens because water molecules have **positive and negative charges,** and they are attracted to the charge on the balloon. Franklin's early studies of electricity helped later scientists understand how electric charges move through different materials, including air and water.

What This Experiment Shows

This simple experiment helps demonstrate some of the same electrical forces that Franklin studied. He didn't have modern tools, but he carefully observed how objects behaved when exposed to electric charges. His experiments led to discoveries about how electricity moves, which eventually led to major inventions like batteries, light bulbs, and electrical circuits.

www.ingramcontent.com/pod-product-compliance
Ingram Content Group UK Ltd.
Pitfield, Milton Keynes, MK11 3LW, UK
UKHW031006240225
455493UK00012B/978

9 798348 514198